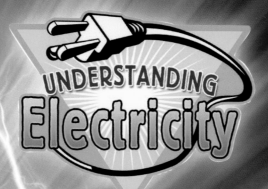
UNDERSTANDING Electricity

What Is Electromagnetism?

Lionel Sandner

Crabtree Publishing Company
www.crabtreebooks.com

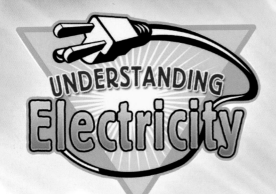

IMPORTANT
All experiments in this book can be conducted by children. When working with electricity, however, it is always recommended that children work with adult supervision.

Author: Lionel Sandner
Publishing plan research and development:
  Sean Charlebois, Reagan Miller
  Crabtree Publishing Company
Project development: Clarity Content Services
Project management: Karen Iversen
Editors: Yvonne Van Ruskenveld, Rachel Eagen
Copy editor: Francine Geraci
Proofreader: Kathy Middleton
Photo research: Linda Tanaka
Design: First Image
Cover design: Margaret Amy Salter, Ken Wright
Production coordinator: Ken Wright
Prepress technician: Ken Wright
Print coordinator: Katherine Berti

Illustrations:
Chandra Ganegoda

Photographs:
cover Thinkstock, shutterstock; p1 scunner/Bigstock; p4 (left) Jupiterimages/Thinkstock, iStockphoto/Thinkstock; p5 Creatas/Thinkstock; p6 left Michael Chamberlin/shutterstock, teravolt/CCL/wiki; p7 top left clockwise Hemera/Thinkstock, Hemera/ Thinkstock, Wormcast/CCL/wiki, Hemera/Thinkstock; p8 left Matthew Cole/iStock, Hemera/Thinkstock; p9 University of Hawaii; p10 Plutonius 3d/shutterstock; p11 (magnet) Brand X Pictures/Thinkstock, (boy) Leah-Anne Thompson/ shutterstock; p12 top Eyecandy Images/ Thinkstock, lower left iStockphoto/Thinkstock, Luis García/CCL/wiki; p13 left Anita Potter/shutterstock, Snowbelle/shutterstock; p14 iStockphoto/Thinkstock; p15 top iStockphoto/ Thinkstock, Smileus/shutterstock, karamysh/shutterstock; p16 iStockphoto/Thinkstock; p17 (top) yampi/shutterstock, (bottom) L Michael Roberts/Wikimedia Commons; p21 GIPhotoStock/ Photo Researchers, Inc.; p22 blanche/shutterstock; p23 Sebcz/dreamstime.com; p25 Ene/dreamstime.com; p26 (left) Comstock Collection/Thinkstock, Jupiterimages/ Thinkstock; p27 Worradirek/dreamstime.com; p28 Nikada/iStockphoto.

Library and Archives Canada Cataloguing in Publication

Sandner, Lionel
    What is electromagnetism? / Lionel Sandner.

(Understanding electricity)
Includes index.
Issued also in electronic format.
ISBN 978-0-7787-2080-5 (bound).--ISBN 978-0-7787-2085-0 (pbk.)

    1. Electromagnetism--Juvenile literature. I. Title.
II. Series: Understanding electricity (St. Catharines, Ont.)

QC760.2.S36 2012   j537   C2012-901506-7

Library of Congress Cataloging-in-Publication Data

Sandner, Lionel.
  What is electromagnetism? / Lionel Sandner.
    p. cm. -- (Understanding electricity)
  Audience: 8-11
  Audience: Grade 4 to 6
  Includes index.
  ISBN 978-0-7787-2080-5 (reinforced lib. bdg. : alk. paper) -- ISBN 978-0-7787-2085-0 (pbk. : alk. paper) -- ISBN 978-1-4271-7940-1 (electronic PDF) -- ISBN 978-1-4271-8055-1 (electronic HTML)
  1. Electromagnetism--Juvenile literature. I. Title.
  QC760.2.S36 2012
  537--dc23
                        2012008265

Crabtree Publishing Company
www.crabtreebooks.com   1-800-387-7650

Printed in the U.S.A./022013/SN20130115

Published in Canada
Crabtree Publishing
616 Welland Ave.
St. Catharines, ON
L2M 5V6

Published in the United States
Crabtree Publishing
PMB 59051
350 Fifth Avenue, 59th Floor
New York, New York 10118

Published in the United Kingdom
Crabtree Publishing
Maritime House
Basin Road North, Hove
BN41 1WR

Published in Australia
Crabtree Publishing
3 Charles Street
Coburg North
VIC 3058

Contents

Be a Magnetism Detective

Have you ever stuck a drawing onto the fridge? Did you use a magnet to do it? Magnets are everywhere you look. You will find them working in hair dryers and electric toothbrushes, and even in the clasps on your jacket.

Magnets connect the engine and cars of this toy train together.

The Many Uses of Magnets

Magnets can be used for many different purposes. They can be used to hold things together, such as on a purse clasp. They can also be used for movement, such as in an electric motor. They can even help to store information on your computer's hard drive. More uses for magnets are being discovered all the time!

Magnets can hold your artwork and schoolwork on the fridge door.

Flash fact

Some paper money is printed with magnetic ink. It makes the money harder to counterfeit, or make a fake copy.

Find the Magnets

If you have ever used magnets, you know they **attract** other items with magnetic **properties**. Are you ready to be a magnet detective? Find a magnet and explore the room you are in. Which items is the magnet attracted to? Make one list of the items that seem to be magnetic and another of the items that do not seem to be magnetic. If you do not have a magnet, take a look at the kitchen in the picture below. What items do you think might be magnetic?

What Is Magnetism?

By now, you have identified some uses of magnets. Have you ever wondered where magnets come from?

Which Metals Are Magnetic?

About 4,000 years ago, a Greek shepherd named Magnes accidentally discovered magnetism. While out tending his sheep, he noticed that the nails in his shoes stuck to one kind of rock. Other people in early Greece and China also recorded their investigations into magnetism. They found that the metal iron would stick to a kind of rock called lodestone.

Lodestone is a natural magnet. Steel nails will stick to it.

Magnets will stick to some metals, but not all of them. The common metals that are magnetic are iron, nickel, and cobalt. Most magnets are made of one or more of these metals. More expensive neodymium magnets are made of materials called rare earth metals.

Types of Magnets

Magnets are made in many different shapes and sizes. The most common forms are shown here. A bar magnet has the shape of a chocolate bar. A horseshoe magnet is a bar magnet bent into the shape of the letter U. Shiny, smaller magnets are neodymium magnets.

Farmers have cows swallow a cow magnet. The magnet sits in the cow's stomach and attracts any magnetic metal the cow may accidentally eat, such as barbed wire. This helps lower the chance of the metal hurting the cow's stomach.

Flash fact

The World of Magnets

Have you ever tried to join two magnets? Sometimes they join tightly. Other times, they will not connect no matter how hard you push. You have discovered one of the characteristics, or properties, of magnets.

Properties of Magnets

All magnets have two ends called poles—a north pole and a south pole. In the illustration on the right, the poles are labeled on the magnets with N for north and S for south.

When the north and south poles of two different magnets come close, they pull toward each other. That is because they are opposites. When two of the same poles, such as two north poles, come close, they **repel**, or push each other away.

Like poles attract each other. Unlike poles repel each other.

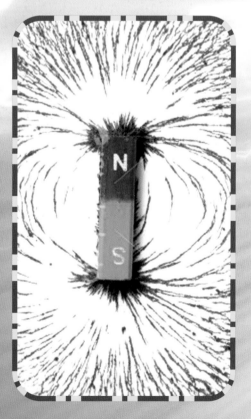

The push or pull between magnets happens when the **magnetic fields** come in contact with each other. A magnetic field is an area around a magnet where the magnetic **force** acts. You can see a magnetic field if you sprinkle iron filings on and around a magnet. Look at this photo of the field around a bar magnet.

- The lines around the magnet show the field. They are called magnetic field lines.
- Each line goes from the north pole to the south pole of the magnet.
- The lines never cross.
- The more magnetic field lines there are in an area, the stronger the magnetic force is.

Try It for Yourself!

Experiment

Make your own magnetic fields.

Materials

- bar magnet
- plastic wrap or clear dish
- iron filings

Procedure

1. Place a sheet of plastic wrap or a clear dish on top of the magnet.
2. Sprinkle iron filings over the plastic sheet or clear dish.
3. Draw what you observe.
4. Try it with two different magnets.

What Happened and Why

All magnets have magnetic fields around them. The iron filings line up along the magnetic field lines.

Measuring Magnetic Strength

This floating globe depends on strong magnets. What gives a magnet its strength?

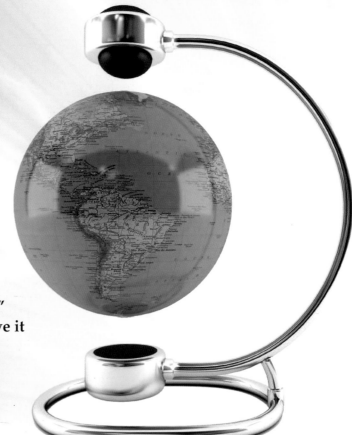

This metal globe "floats" between magnets, one above it and one below it.

Magnetic Strength

  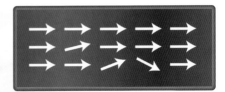

The magnet with the most arrows lined up in the same direction is the strongest.

Magnets come in various strengths. Think of a magnet as being made up of many tiny, weak magnets. The more of the tiny magnets that line up in the same direction, the stronger the big magnet is. There are three iron bars in the image above. In each bar, the tiny magnets are represented by arrows. Scientists refer to these tiny magnets as **domains**. In the image, the bar on the left is nonmagnetic, the bar in the middle is weakly magnetic, and the bar on the right is strongly magnetic. In other words, the more domains that line up in the same direction, the stronger the magnet.

Try It for Yourself!

Experiment

Now it is your chance to test some magnets to see which is the strongest.

Procedure

1. Make a pile of 30 to 40 paper clips.
2. Take a magnet and dip it into the paper clip pile.
3. Remove the magnet from the pile.
4. Pull off and count how many paper clips stuck to the magnet. Write the number on a piece of paper.
5. Repeat with a different magnet.
6. Which magnet do you think is stronger?

What Happened and Why

Stronger magnets are able to pick up more objects or bigger objects. They can do this because they have more domains that line up than weaker magnets.

What Is a Compass?

Hundreds of years ago, explorers sailed all over the world with only a compass **to guide them.**

The First Compasses

Early Greek and Chinese sailors discovered an important use for magnets. They attached a small magnet to a piece of cork and placed it in a bowl of water. They found that the magnet always made the cork point north. The explorers realized that this discovery would help them find their way at sea wherever they went.

Over time, different compasses were designed using materials other than cork. No matter what the design, the compass has always allowed travelers to find their way home.

Did you know that a compass is a floating magnet?

Ships' captains used this Spanish compass over 300 years ago.

This ancient Chinese compass is over 2,000 years old. The spoon is magnetic because it is made of lodestone. It points north like the needle on a compass.

The Earth's Magnetic Field

Think of the Earth as a large magnet. A giant magnetic field called the **magnetosphere** surrounds the Earth. Scientists think this magnetism is caused by the molten or liquid iron around Earth's solid center. The molten iron moves slowly, and this creates a very weak magnetic field.

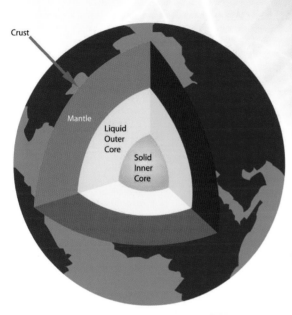

Earth has a molten layer of iron that moves slowly around its solid inner core.

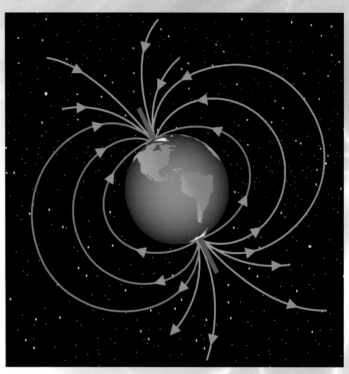

Earth is a giant magnet with a magnetic field surrounding it in space.

A compass is a detector of very weak magnetic fields. When you hold a compass, the needle lines up along one of Earth's magnetic field lines, always pointing north.

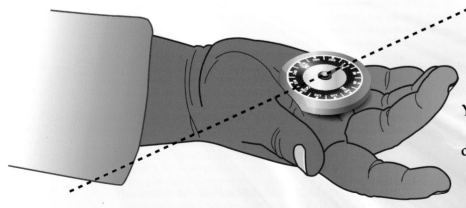

You cannot see the Earth's magnetic field, but your compass lines up with the lines in the field.

Magnetism in the Natural World

One clear winter night you look up into the sky. There you see sheets of light that look like colored curtains floating high above you. The red, green, and yellow curtains seem to move. If you listen closely, you hear a crackling sound in the air. What is it?

The northern lights may be all one color or several colors.

Magnetism Above Us

If you have witnessed this phenomenon, you have seen the northern lights or **aurora borealis**. This is one of nature's most spectacular light shows. Earth is constantly being bombarded by charged particles from the sun. When these electrically charged particles, or tiny pieces of matter, hit Earth's magnetic field, they give off light.

Flash fact

Earth's magnetic field helps protect us from harmful particles emitted by the sun. It prevents these particles from reaching Earth's surface.

Animal Magnetism

How does a bird navigate when it flies south for the winter? How does a honeybee find its way back to the hive? They both use magnets!

Research has shown that birds, such as robins, have a built-in compass that helps them to sense magnetic fields. This compass helps them orient themselves, or find the right direction, by using Earth's magnetic field. Bees also have an inner compass that helps them return to the hive.

Robins have special vision that actually helps them "see" Earth's magnetic fields. This helps guide them while flying.

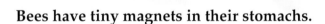

Bees have tiny magnets in their stomachs.

Robins and bees are not the only creatures with built-in compasses. Fish have them, too! The yellowfin tuna, Atlantic salmon, and rainbow trout all have magnetic crystals in their bodies that help them navigate.

The magnetic crystals in salmon act as compasses to guide them.

What Is Electricity?

A flash of lightning, turning on your bedroom lights, and listening to music on your music player are all familiar examples of electricity use. Electricity is the buildup or flow of charged particles called electrons. Electrons have a negative charge.

Conductors Transport Electricity

Conductors are materials that electricity can easily pass through. A metal wire is an example of a conductor. In your home, electrical wires are covered in plastic, which is an **insulator**. Insulators are materials that do not allow electricity to flow through them.

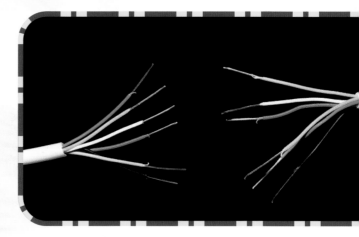

The plastic insulation around wire is an insulator. It protects us from the electricity flowing through the wire, or conductor.

Current electricity is a flow of electrons. The current carries the electrical energy needed to run an electrical device.

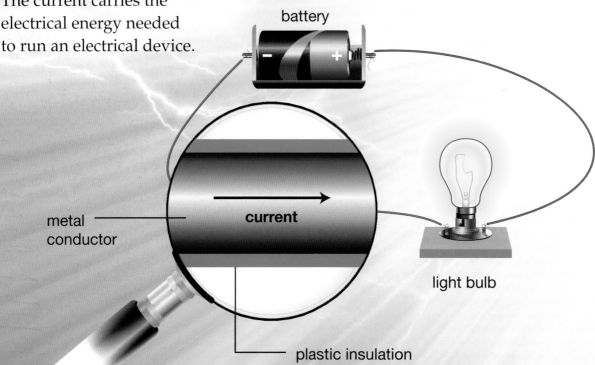

battery

metal conductor — current

light bulb

plastic insulation

Using Electrical Energy

Every electrical device needs a supply of electrical energy to operate. Electrical devices convert this energy into other forms of energy. For example, a light bulb converts electrical energy into light and heat. A toaster converts electrical energy into heat that cooks the toast.

The element, or burner, on this stove converts electrical energy to heat energy and light energy.

Batteries contain a chemical mixture that allows them to store electrical energy. They are commonly used in portable electronic devices, such as MP3 players.

Magnetic induction lamps use electromagnets to create a strong magnetic field. This causes a small, solid piece of mercury inside the bulb to glow.

Flash fact

What Is Electromagnetism?

Observing something you do not expect to see can lead to an exciting surprise. That is exactly what happened to a science teacher in Denmark in 1820.

An Accidental Event

While teaching his class, Hans Christian Oersted brought a compass close to a wire carrying an electrical current. He noticed that the compass needle moved. This made him curious and led him to experiment further. Oersted's investigation revealed the results below.

He found that when a wire holding an electrical current is placed in line with the north point of the compass, the compass needle moves **perpendicular** to the wire. This happens only when there is an electrical current in the wire. Oersted did not realize he had just made a very important discovery.

No electric current is moving through the wire.

Electric current moves through the wire. The compass needle moves to become perpendicular to the wire.

The Electricity and Magnetism Connection

Oersted's discovery was important because he showed the connection between electricity and magnetism. The compass needle moved when it got near a wire carrying an electrical current because there was a magnetic field around the wire. Oersted concluded that the magnetic field occurred only when there was a current in the wire. This meant people could control when a magnetic field could be turned on and off!

A compass needle moves perpendicular to a wire carrying an electrical current because of the magnetic field created by the current.

What Is an Electromagnet?

Oersted's discovery eventually led to the invention of the electromagnet. An electromagnet is a magnet made by using the magnetic field around a wire carrying an electrical current.

How Does an Electromagnet Work?

The picture below shows the parts of an electromagnet. A copper wire is wrapped into a coil around a core, or central tube. The ends of the wire are attached to a battery. A **switch** turns the electrical current off or on by opening or closing the **circuit**.

When the current is on, the coil generates a magnetic field like the one around a bar magnet. It has north and south poles. The strongest parts of the magnetic field are at the poles. An electromagnet is called a temporary magnet because it is a magnet only when the current is flowing.

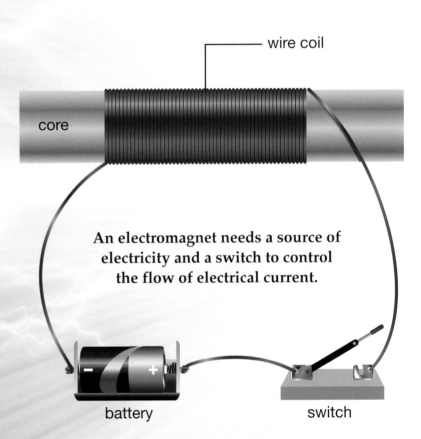

wire coil

core

An electromagnet needs a source of electricity and a switch to control the flow of electrical current.

battery   switch

Flash fact

The strongest magnets in the world are electromagnets.

Try It for Yourself!

Experiment

Build your own electromagnet.

Materials

- wire
- battery
- iron nail
- toilet paper tube
- pencil
- compass
- paper clips

Procedure

1. Wrap the wire around the pencil as many times as you can.
2. Attach the ends of the wire to a battery. This is your electromagnet.
3. Bring the compass close to the electromagnet's poles and sides. Write down what you see.
4. Place your electromagnet near a pile of paper clips. How many paper clips were you able to pick up?
5. Unplug your electromagnet by detaching the wires from the battery.
6. Follow the same steps using an iron nail, then a toilet paper tube. See how many paper clips each can pick up using each one as the core.
7. Unplug your electromagnet when you are finished.

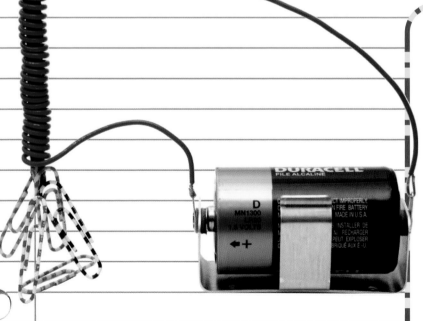

What Happened and Why

Coiling the wire around an iron core created an electromagnet. The toilet paper tube does not contain a magnetic property and so could not work. The lead in a pencil is not a strong enough metal to make an electromagnet work.

To make an electromagnet stronger, you can add more turns in the coil or increase the current.

Electromagnets in Your Home

Walk around your home. Make a list of all the devices that use electromagnetism. How many did you find? Did you find ones like the devices shown on this page?

An electromagnet is part of the motor that moves air through the hair dryer.

The electromagnet in your doorbell is wired into an electric circuit in your house.

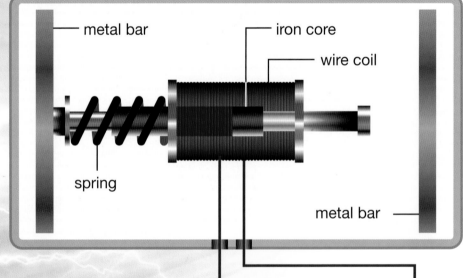

metal bar   iron core

wire coil

spring

metal bar

Ring My Bell

How does a doorbell make a sound when you push a button? The doorbell is a combination of an electrical circuit and an electromagnet. When you push the doorbell button, an electromagnet pulls on a metal bar that then hits a bell. You hear the bell and take your finger off the button. The metal bar returns to its normal position.

PRESS

Electromagnets at Home

Many doors require keys to unlock them, but new doors with keypads are now being used. A code is entered to activate a temporary electrical current, which acts as an electromagnet to pull the lock open.

Do you enjoy listening to music? Both speakers and headphones use electromagnets, which help to convert electrical energy into music signals that you can hear. The sounds you hear result from the movement, or vibration, of a cone that sits inside the speaker.

The electromagnet inside the door lock means you do not have to use a key.

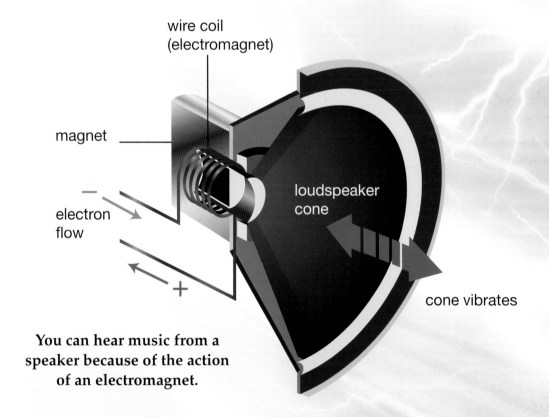

wire coil (electromagnet)

magnet

electron flow

loudspeaker cone

cone vibrates

You can hear music from a speaker because of the action of an electromagnet.

Electromagnets in Your Life

Strong winds have knocked out power lines, and you have no electricity at your school. Luckily, the principal has a backup plan. A gas-powered generator is used to provide enough electricity to keep the lights and heat on in the school.

How Does a Generator Work?

A moving wire in a magnetic field can generate electricity. A generator has a coil of wire called a **rotor**. The rotor spins around in the magnetic field of a **permanent magnet**. When it spins, a force acts on the charges in the wire coil. This results in an electrical current.

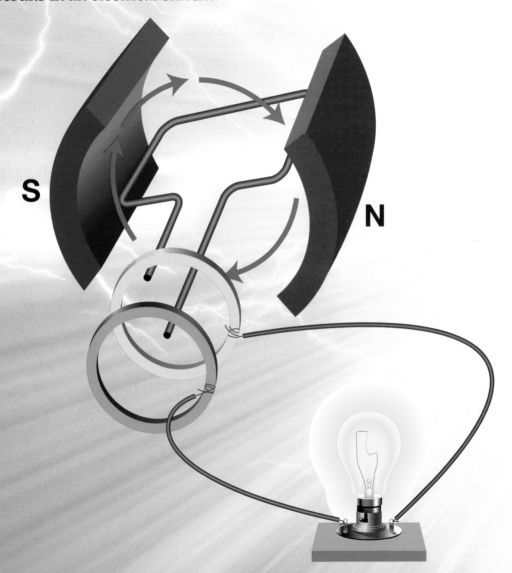

Generators and Motors

Large generators at power plants have machines with blades called **turbines**. Pressure from water or steam turns the blades of the turbines, creating electricity for use in our homes and schools.

A motor is designed like a generator, but it produces mechanical (motion) energy rather than electrical energy. The spinning motion produced by the motor is used to turn the wheels of an electric car or bicycle, or the blades of an electric lawnmower.

It is easy to go fast when there's an electric motor to give you a boost!

electric motor

Flash fact

The world's smallest motor is 1 nanometer wide. A human hair is 60,000 nanometers wide.

Electromagnets in the World

You will find many other applications of electromagnetism all around you. Some you may know and others may surprise you.

Looking Inside

If you are sick, your doctor may ask for a picture that uses electromagnets! You walk into a room and a large machine like the one shown here is in front of you. It looks like a space vehicle. It is called a magnetic resonance imaging scanner (MRI). It uses electromagnets to scan your body. These large electromagnets are in the cylinder surrounding the bed in the picture. An MRI scan shows the soft tissues of your body.

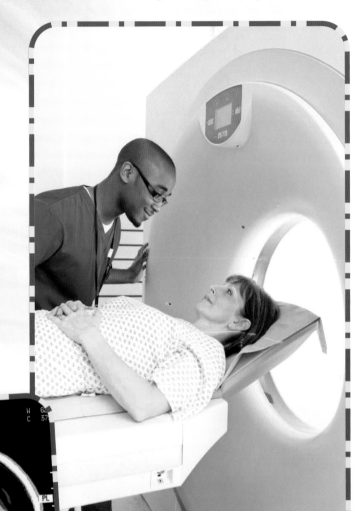

An MRI machine can scan the whole body.

This MRI scan shows a cross-section of a brain. The image helps doctors identify tumors or other health issues.

Recycling Cars with Electromagnets

When a car stops working, it is sent to a junkyard. At the junkyard the car is broken apart. The parts are separated out by a huge electromagnet for recycling. The chart below shows how much of a car can be recycled.

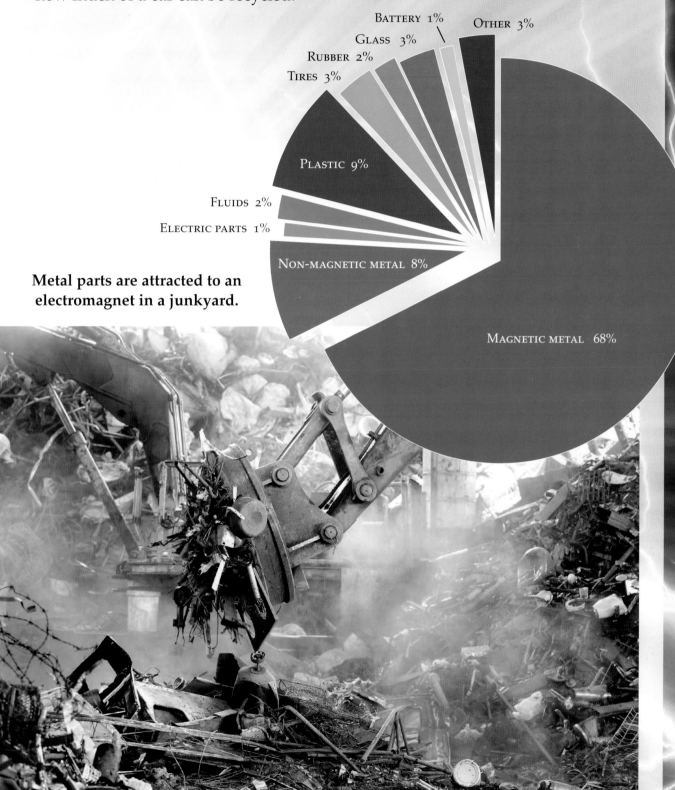

Metal parts are attracted to an electromagnet in a junkyard.

BATTERY 1%

GLASS 3%

RUBBER 2%

OTHER 3%

TIRES 3%

PLASTIC 9%

FLUIDS 2%

ELECTRIC PARTS 1%

NON-MAGNETIC METAL 8%

MAGNETIC METAL 68%

Electromagnets in the Future

Here are some wild and wonderful uses of electromagnetism that may be new to you.

Trains That Float

Most trains travel on wheels but some trains move by floating! In Japan, China, and Europe, MAGLEV trains use electromagnetism to travel at very high speeds. Imagine electromagnets lined up along a track and a train with electromagnets underneath it. Both have the same poles facing each other. This makes the train float or levitate about 0.5 inch to 4 inches (about 1 to 10 cm) above the rail. With no friction between wheels and track, the train can travel over 300 mph (500 km/h). This is about half the speed of a passenger jet!

MAGLEV stands for magnetic levitation. Levitation means floating.

Cool Magnets

At very cold temperatures, some materials can conduct electricity with no resistance. These materials are called superconductors. Superconducting magnets are electromagnets made of superconducting wire. They are used in scientific research and some medical imaging.

Electromagnets to the Stars

Imagine launching into space without a rocket engine to propel you. This is exactly what NASA hopes to do with an electromagnetic launcher called a railgun. This development could usher in a new era for space exploration in the future.

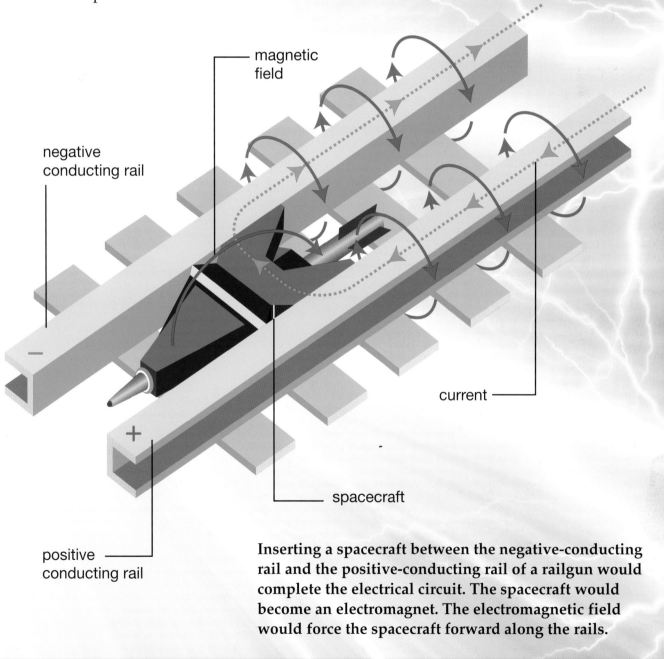

negative conducting rail

magnetic field

current

spacecraft

positive conducting rail

Inserting a spacecraft between the negative-conducting rail and the positive-conducting rail of a railgun would complete the electrical circuit. The spacecraft would become an electromagnet. The electromagnetic field would force the spacecraft forward along the rails.

Glossary

attract   Pull toward

aurora borealis   Northern lights, caused by charged particles from the sun hitting Earth's atmosphere

battery   A container filled with a chemical mixture that can produce electricity

circuit   A circular route that returns to its starting point

compass   A small, floating magnet that points north

conductor   Material that electricity can pass through

current electricity   Flowing electrons

domain   A part of a magnet acting like a mini-magnet

electromagnet   A magnet created by electricity flowing through wire

electron   A negative particle circling an atom's nucleus

force   A push or pull

generator   A machine that produces electrical current

insulator   Material that electricity cannot pass through

magnetic field   The area of magnetic force around a magnet

magnetosphere   Giant magnetic field around Earth

permanent magnet   An object that is magnetized and has a stable magnetic field

perpendicular   A line at a right angle to another line

property   A characteristic; helps describe a material and make it different from other things

repel   Push apart

rotor   Coil of wire that spins around in the magnetic field of a permanent magnet in a generator

switch   A device used to open or close a circuit

turbine   A bladed machine that spins when force is applied

Learning More

FURTHER READING

Hydroelectric Power: Power from Moving Water (Energy Revolution). Marguerite Rodger. Crabtree Publishing, 2010.

Inventing the Electric Light (Breakthrough Inventions). Lisa Mullins. Crabtree Publishing, 2007.

Using Energy (Green Team). Sally Hewitt. Crabtree Publishing, 2008.

What Are Electrical Circuits? (Understanding Electricity). Ronald Monroe. Crabtree Publishing, 2012.

What Are Insulators and Conductors? (Understanding Electricity). Jessica Pegis. Crabtree Publishing, 2012.

What Is Electricity? (Understanding Electricity). Ronald Monroe. Crabtree Publishing, 2012.

WEBSITES

Explain That Stuff!
www.explainthatstuff.com/magnetism.html

exploratorium
www.exploratorium.edu/snacks/magnetic_lines

How Stuff Works
www.howstuffworks.com/electromagnet.htm

neoK12 Electricity
www.neok12.com/Electromagnetism.htm

Science Kids
www.sciencekids.co.nz/videos/physics/magnets.html

Index